WATER KEFIR

Caleb Warnock

THE BACKYARD RENAISSANCE COLLECTION

DISCOVER THE LONG-LOST SKILLS OF SELF-RELIANCE

My name is Caleb Warnock, and I've been working for years to learn how to return to forgotten skills, the skills of our ancestors. As our world becomes increasingly unstable, self-reliance becomes invaluable. Throughout this series, *The Backyard Renaissance*, I will share with you the lost skills of self-sufficiency and healthy living. Come with me and other do-it-yourself experimenters, and rediscover the joys and successes of simple self-reliance.

FAMILIUS

Published by Familius LLC, www.familius.com

Familius books are available at special discounts for bulk purchases for sales promotions or for family or corporate use. Special editions, including personalized covers, excerpts of existing books, or books with corporate logos, can be created in large quantities for special needs. For more information, contact Premium Sales at 559-876-2170 or email specialmarkets@familius.com.

Library of Congress Catalog-in-Publication Data
2016961878
ISBN 9781944822682

Edited by Maggie Wickes
Cover design by David Miles
Book design by David Miles and Maggie Wickes

10 9 8 7 6 5 4 3 2 1
First Edition

CONTENTS

INTRODUCTION.. VII

BENEFITS OF HOMEMADE WATER KEFIR............................1

INSTRUCTIONS FOR USING WATER KEFIR GRAINS........ 11

RECIPES 15

QUESTIONS & ANSWERS...19

ADDITIONAL RESEARCH SOURCES: 25

ABOUT THE AUTHOR.. 27

INTRODUCTION

When it comes to our health, we have two choices. We can use perpetual probiotics to make ourselves healthy, or we can eat a poor diet to make ourselves perpetually and chronically sick. We are surrounded by legions of people who have made themselves perpetually sick by eating little fiber, no live probiotics, and a diet poor in amino acids. Health is created by eating natural live probiotics with protein and whole grains (properly treated with natural yeast) to provide nutrition and fiber. A balanced diet is necessary for all the amino acids our body must have to create and replenish the cells in our body. The body can only work with the nutritional tools we give it. When we do not eat correctly, we become sick. When we make a habit of eating poorly, we become chronically and perpetually sick with autoimmune disorders, mutations, edema, and permanent tissue damage. We also allow bad bacteria to colonize our gut. We have breathing disorders and severe allergies.

In plain language, we can make ourselves well. We can eat our way to health!

Water kefir grains are used to make a probiotic all-natural drink. The grains eat sugar as their food and produce beneficial bacteria and yeasts needed for healthy human digestion. Fresh grains can be ordered from SeedRenaissance.com. They are shipped fresh, in dechlorinated water with honey, in a sealed foil envelope, and need to be strained and given clean water and honey or other sugar at your home soon after you receive them. Water kefir grains look like colorless chunks of gummy candy. Water kefir is a naturally occurring mass of all-natural, beneficial bacteria and yeasts. The grains are added to water mixed with a small amount of honey to make a drink that is powerfully healthy and probiotic and has been used for centuries.

Water kefir is a perpetual probiotic—perpetual meaning never ending. Water kefir grains are perpetual because you can literally use them to make all the kefired water you want for the rest of your life. Water kefir grains are naturally abundant, meaning that they are part of the natural law of abundance. Nature is self-sustaining and, when taken care of properly, provides what is necessary.

BENEFITS OF HOMEMADE WATER KEFIR

- Natural source of living probiotics to regulate and heal the gut
- Naturally fights allergies, asthma, and autoimmune disorders
- Inhibits colitis, cancer, and many other diseases
- Water kefir grains are a true perpetual culture. You can use them for a lifetime
- Can be used to make healthy drinks and can be added to recipes and other water-based foods
- Is lactose-free
- Is gluten-free

HEALTH BENEFITS OF WATER KEFIR

ater kefir grains are made up of naturally occurring bacteria and yeasts that have symbiotic relationships with each other. These beneficial bacteria and yeasts act both directly and indirectly to boost the immune system, decrease asthma, fight infection and colonization of bad bacteria in our digestive tract, fight cancer cells, and many other health effects. The science also shows us that water kefir provides health benefits you cannot get from other probiotics, and that because some of the beneficial bacteria in water kefir are not able to colonize the gut, we need to regularly consume water kefir and other probiotics for our best health.

According to a 2011 study in the *International Journal of Food Microbiology*, water kefir grains contain the following probiotic strains of beneficial bacteria and yeasts:

BACTERIA SPECIES

- *Lactobacillus brevis*
- *Lactobacillus casei*
- *Lactobacillus hilgardii*
- *Lactobacillus hordei*
- *Lactobacillus nagelii*
- *Leuconostoc citreum*
- *Leuconostoc mesenteroides*

- *Acetobacter fabarum*
- *Acetobacter orientalis*
- *Streptococcus lactis*

YEAST SPECIES

- Hanseniaspora valbyensis
- Lachancea fermentati
- Saccharomyces cerevisiae
- Zygotorulaspora florentina

Source: www.ufrb.edu.br/kefirdoreconcavo/images/A_diversidade_microbiana_do_kefir_de_água.pdf

Scientific research confirms that these probiotic bacteria and yeasts in kefir grains have at least twenty proven health-promoting properties:

1. Certain probiotic strains can either form or increase vitamins in food.

2. Certain probiotic strains have the ability to help curb or kill bad bacteria or help the body restrain bad bacteria.

3. Probiotic strains contain bioactive peptides—chains of amino acids which perform many specific functions to help the body moderate and increase health.

Consuming water kefir helps to make these available to your body.

4. Probiotic strains contain exopolysaccharides—metabolites produced by probiotic bacteria that the body needs to moderate nutrition and keep the functions of the body balanced.

5. Some probiotic strains, including those in water kefir, have been show to help the body fight off and reduce chronic inflammation. Chronic swelling, which is also called inflammation or edema, in the tissues of the body can have a huge number of negative health effects.

6. New studies have shown that consuming certain probiotics, including those found in water kefir, can "alleviate the risks of certain types of cancers."

7. New studies have shown that consuming certain probiotics, including those found in water kefir, can "suppress colonic tumor incidence, volume and multiplicity induced by various carcinogens in different animal models." In addition, these cultures,

when administered to animals in studies, inhibited liver, colon, bladder, and mammary tumors, highlighting the potential for probiotics to improve human health.

8
Probiotics inhibit pathogens. Pathogens are any microorganisms, including bacteria and viruses, that cause disease. Put in plain language, science has shown that drinking water kefir helps us avoid disease in our bodies.

9
Probiotics heal leaky gut syndrome. Probiotics help regulate and increase the lining of the small intestine, which is hugely important for keeping bad bacteria out of the bloodstream and the body.

10
Probiotics enhance and heal the intestinal barrier. Our intestines are lined with a single-cell layer called the epithelium that constitutes the largest and most important barrier against the external environment. It acts as a selectively permeable barrier permitting the absorption of nutrients, electrolytes, and water, while maintaining an effective defense against toxins, antigens, and harmful bacteria. Over the past

decade, there has been increasing recognition of an association between disrupted intestinal barrier function and the development of autoimmune and inflammatory diseases. Intestinal epithelial barrier dysfunction is a major factor contributing to the predisposition to inflammatory diseases including food allergy, inflammatory bowel disease, and celiac disease.

11

Probiotics boost immune response. Diet directly affects the ability of our bodies to fend off outside intruders (pathogens) that would cause disease. There is mounting evidence that our gut microbiota is a virtual endocrine organ which plays a direct role in producing and regulating naturally occurring compounds that reach the circulation and act to influence the function of distal organs and body systems.

12

Probiotics in the gut allow our bodies to synthesize vitamins and metabolize bile acids, sterols, and xenobiotics. The beneficial bacteria in water kefir helps our body to safely process foreign pollutants including drugs, synthetic pesticides, herbicides, and industrial pollutants.

13 Probiotics have antimutagenic effects against a range of mutagens and promutagens. Mutagens are substances that disrupt or change the genes of an organism. Mutagens are often cancerous.

14 Probiotics reduce the risk of colorectal cancer.

15 Probiotics reduce the risk for cardiovascular diseases

16 Homemade fresh water kefir is healthier and more active than commercially produced powdered and freeze-dried probiotics because of lengthy storage.

17 There is a direct decrease in allergies when we consume water kefir and other probiotics.

18 Science has shown us that the good bacteria in water kefir can act directly to decrease asthma.

19 Colitis disease is a chronic inflammation of the colon wall which can cause painful ulcers and other damage to the colon. Water kefir helps prevent and potentially heal colitis.

20 Probiotics contribute to improved gastrointesinal

functioning. When we do not process food correctly, all manner of diseases, pain, and health issues can follow. Most of us need help improving our gut function because of antibiotics, chlorinated water, antibiotics in our meat, lack of soluble and insoluble dietary fiber, overabundance of sugar, and other factors that decrease the ability of our gut to function properly.

SOURCES:

http://www.ncbi.nlm.nih.gov/pmc/articles/PMC4566036/
http://www.ncbi.nlm.nih.gov/pubmed/27020288
http://www.horizonpress.com/lactobacillus
http://journals.plos.org/plosone/article?id=10.1371/journal.pone.0139910
http://journals.plos.org/plosone/article?id=10.1371/journal.pone.0078789
http://www.ncbi.nlm.nih.gov/pmc/articles/PMC4266989/
http://www.ncbi.nlm.nih.gov/pmc/articles/PMC3983973/
https://www.ncbi.nlm.nih.gov/pubmed/24892638?dopt=Abstract

WHERE TO GET FRESH WATER KEFIR GRAINS

I own SeedRenaissance.com, and I ship live water kefir grains (and a variety of other probiotic cultures) all over the United States. To my knowledge, my company is the only one which sells living water kefir grains instead of dried or freeze-dried water kefir grains. Each package comes with full instructions.

INSTRUCTIONS FOR USING WATER KEFIR GRAINS

STEP 1: Open the sealed foil envelope and carefully pour the contents into a fine mesh strainer, sieve, sieve cloth, coffee filter, or cheesecloth. The grains may have a sour smell depending on how long they have been in shipping. This sour smell is temporary. The water in the envelope may appear to be carbonated. This is a natural effect of water kefir grains. Using cold tap water, wash the grains. *Be careful* not to wash your kefir grains down the sink.

STEP 2: To feed your water kefir grains, you will need non-chlorinated water. You can buy purified water at the grocery store or let tap water sit in an open jar for 48 hours, covered with cloth to keep out dust. Place your water kefir grains in a glass mason jar. Pour non-chlorinated water (cold or room temperature) into the jar. Add a volume of honey, molasses, agave, coconut sugar, or any other form of sugar (not sugar substitute) to the water that is equal to *half the volume* of the kefir grains you have. This means that if you have a teaspoon of kefir grains, you will need to add a half teaspoon of sugar. If you have a quarter cup of water kefir grains, you will need to add a 1/8 cup of the sugar of your choice. Stirring is not necessary.

STEP 3: Put the lid loosely on the jar unless you are an experienced water kefir maker and wish to make a carbonated drink (more on this later). Leave the jar on your kitchen counter for at least 48 hours. The beneficial bacterias and yeast in the kefir grains are mesophilic, meaning they only grow at moderate temperatures. Refrigerating the grains will immediately stop them from turning the sugar into a probiotic sugar-free drink. You must *not* refrigerate the jar until the grains have eaten all the sugar *do not* shake or move the jar.

STEP 4: You will know the kefir is finished when you can occasionally see small bubbles floating from the grains at the bottom of the jar to the top of the jar. If you do not see bubbles and your water kefir jar has been at room temperature for more than 72 hours, your water kefir should be finished. Taste the water kefir. Strain out the grains, and add non-chlorinated water and your choice of sugar to them to start a new batch of water kefir. Use the kefired water to drink plain, make flavored punches and other drinks, or add to green smoothies.

STORING WATER KEFIR GRAINS

If you want to take a break from "tending" your water kefir grains, put them in a clean glass jar with non-chlorinated water and the sugar of your choice, and leave them out until the water turns to water kefir. Put the whole jar into the fridge, with the lid on, until you are ready to make more kefir. The grains will store like this (in the finished kefir) for months, but the water inside the jar will slowly turn sour. When you are ready to make new water kefir, strain out the grains, discard the sour water, and then feed the grains to make new kefir by following the instructions above. You can keep kefired water in the fridge for days. You can also keep it at room temperature, but it will sour.

RECIPES

LEMON LIMEADE

Makes one gallon.

Stevia is an herb with sugar-flavored leaves. This recipe uses the sweet extract of stevia, which you can purchase online and at health food stores.

Cold water kefir (with grains strained out) and ice (1 total gallon)
2 tablespoons + 2 teaspoons lime juice
2 tablespoons + 2 teaspoons lemon juice
1 teaspoon powdered stevia extract, 90 percent strength
1/3 cup powdered sugar substitute (recipe found in *The Stevia Solution*)

 Stir together and serve.

STEVIA APPLE JUICE

Makes 1 quart; can be doubled.

3 medium to large apples, cleaned
2 cups cold water kefir
2 measured smidgens pure powdered stevia extract, 90
    percent strength
2 more cups cold water kefir
Sieve cloth or strainer

 Quarter the apples, then cut the quarters in half.

 Put 2 cups water kefir in a blender. On the "blend" setting, add the apple pieces one at a time until all the apples are blended.

 Put your strainer or sieve cloth over a pitcher and pour in the blended apple mixture. Press the apples in the strainer or sieve cloth to get all the juice.

 Add the remaining two cups of water kefir. Stir and refrigerate if desired.

WATER KEFIR GRAPE JUICE

Makes 1 quart; can be doubled.

> 1 1/2 cups clean sweet grapes, rinsed and stems removed
> 2 cups cold water kefir, grains removed
> 2 measured smidgens pure powdered stevia extract, 90 percent strength
> 2 more cups cold water kefir, grains removed
> Sieve cloth or strainer

1. Combine the grapes and 2 cups water kefir in the blender. Use the "blend" setting until all the grapes are blended.

2. Put your strainer or sieve cloth over a pitcher and pour in the blended grape mixture.

3. Add the remaining 2 cups of water kefir. Stir and refrigerate if desired.

QUESTIONS & ANSWERS

Question: Do the kefir grains grow?

Answer: Yes. Water kefir grains double in size roughly every ten feedings (ten times you let them make kefir). The more water kefir grains you have in your jar, the faster they will make kefir. If you have extra grains, you can give them away, compost them, or feed them to your chickens.

Question: Can I eat the kefir grains?

Answer: Yes, they are safe to eat, but they don't have much flavor and are chewy. However, if you eat all your grains, you won't be able to make more kefir.

Question: How many kefir grains do I need to make kefir?

Answer: You can make kefir with any amount of grains. If you have less than a quarter cup of grains, it could take many days to make a gallon of water kefir at a time.

Question: I was told I should shake my kefir jar once or twice a day. Why don't you recommend this?

Answer: Water kefir grains naturally carbonate the water they are in over time. If the lid is tight on the jar, shaking the jar could cause the jar to fizz or even pop. On rare occasions, with a very tight jar, the jar could explode if the kefir grains have been inside long enough, whether you shake the jar or not. Never shake the jar, and always leave the lid loose. If you are using a canning jar lid, place it upside down to keep the rubber gasket from sealing.

Question: Are water kefir grains and milk kefir grains the same thing? Can I use them interchangeably?

Answer: No. Water kefir grains will not turn milk to kefir, and milk kefir grains will not turn water to kefir.

Question: Can I use my water kefir grains to make homemade root beer, homemade citrus soda, and other carbonated drinks?

Answer: Yes, if you are careful. As explained earlier, water kefir grains can cause a glass jar to explode (just like homemade root beer jars made with yeast sometimes explode) if the pressure builds up too high as the kefir grains eat the sugar and produce a byproduct of carbon dioxide. Carbonated drinks are traditionally made with water kefir by hand-tightening a canning lid on the jar. Once the lid pops up and goes hard in the center, you must open the jar within twelve hours (slowly and carefully, with the lid covered by a cloth towel and pointing away from your face). Never tap a canning jar with a hard lid that has popped up in the center, as it may explode. If you cannot open the jar by hand at this point, put the jar into a garbage bag and discard it in your outdoor trashcan, because it is too dangerous to open (the glass jar may explode). If you are not confident that you can make homemade, naturally carbonated yeast or kefir drink safely, you should never attempt the process.

Question: Is carbonization necessary for the kefired water to be fully finished? If it is not carbonated, is it still healthy and probiotic?

Answer: Carbonization is not necessary when making kefired water. Using water kefir with a loose lid, or covering the jar with cheesecloth or fabric instead of a lid, does not decrease the health benefits of the kefir. It simply allows the natural carbon dioxide produced by the yeasts in the water kefir grains to dissipate harmlessly.

Question: Does my finished water kefir contain alcohol?

Answer: It might contain traces after 48 hours. You can make beer with water kefir grains. Making beer and other alcoholic beverages from water kefir requires specific timing and preparation.

Question: You suggest feeding the water kefir grains honey, but other sources online say this is not recommended. Why?

Answer: Water kefir grains grow more slowly in honey than they do in processed sugar. This may be because honey is comprised of more than one type of naturally occurring sugar and the grains may prefer one kind more than another. As long as you use raw, pure, organic honey, you should be fine. My water kefir grains are happy and healthy and have been for years, so feeding them honey seems to have no negative effect on the grains.

Question: Exactly what probiotic strains are found in water kefir grains?

Answer: Water kefir contains far more probiotic strains than yogurt or most store-bought probiotics that are dried. In the research section of this book, there is a list of strains found by one study, but it is important to know that water kefir probiotic strains vary widely depending on the region of origin and how they are treated. This is a natural part of Mother Nature's diversity.

Other questions? Email calebwarnock@yahoo.com :) Enjoy!

ADDITIONAL RESEARCH SOURCES:

Horisberger, M., 1969. Structure of the dextran of the tibi grain. *Carbohydrate Research* 10, 379–385.

Franzetti, L., Galli, A., Pagani, M.A., de Noni, I., 1998. Microbiological and chemical investigations on "Sugar Kefir" drink. *Annali di Microbiologia ed Enzimologia* 48, 67–80.

Neve, H., Heller, K.J., 2002. The microflora of water kefir: a glance by scanning electron microscopy. *Kieler Milchwirtschaftliche Forschungsberichte* 54, 337–349.

Pidoux, M., 1989. The microbial flora of sugary kefir grain (the gingerbeer plant): biosynthesis of the grain from *Lactobacillus hilgardii* producing a polysaccharide gel. *MIRCEN Journal* 5, 223–238.

Pidoux, M., Brillouet, J.M., Quermener, B., 1988. Characterization of the polysaccharides from a *Lactobacillus brevis* and from sugary kefir grains. *Biotechnology Letters* 10 (6), 415–420.

ABOUT THE AUTHOR

aleb Warnock is the popular author of eighteen books, including *Forgotten Skills of Self-Sufficiency Used by the Mormon Pioneers, The Art of Baking with Natural Yeast, Backyard Winter Gardening for All Climates, More Forgotten Skills*, and the Backyard Renaissance Collection. He is the owner of SeedRenaissance.com, where you can sign up for his email newsletters. Find his Youtube channel at http://bit.ly/1OevHxT

ABOUT FAMILIUS

Welcome to a place where mothers are celebrated, not compared. Where heart is at the center of our families, and family at the center of our homes. Where boo boos are still kissed, cake beaters are still licked, and mistakes are still okay. Welcome to a place where books—and family—are beautiful. Familius: a book publisher dedicated to helping families be happy.

VISIT OUR WEBSITE: WWW.FAMILIUS.COM

Our website is a different kind of place. Get inspired, read articles, discover books, watch videos, connect with our family experts, download books and apps and audiobooks, and along the way, discover how values and happy family life go together.

JOIN OUR FAMILY

There are lots of ways to connect with us! Subscribe to our newsletters at www.familius.com to receive uplifting daily inspiration, essays from our Pater Familius, a free ebook every month, and the first word on special discounts and Familius news.

BECOME AN EXPERT

Familius authors and other established writers interested in helping families be happy are invited to join our family and contribute online content. If you have something important to say on the family, join our expert community by applying at:

www.familius.com/apply-to-become-a-familius-expert

GET BULK DISCOUNTS

If you feel a few friends and family might benefit from what you've read, let us know and we'll be happy to provide you with quantity discounts. Simply email us at specialorders@familius.com.

Website: www.familius.com
Facebook: www.facebook.com/paterfamilius
Twitter: @familiustalk, @paterfamilius1
Pinterest: www.pinterest.com/familius

THE MOST IMPORTANT WORK YOU EVER DO WILL BE WITHIN THE WALLS OF YOUR OWN HOME.

ightning Source UK Ltd.
filton Keynes UK
KOW02f1848010317
°5676UK00001B/1/P